5|18

Becoming a Salamander

by Grace Hansen

Abdo
CHANGING ANIMALS
Kids

abdopublishing.com

Published by Abdo Kids, a division of ABDO, PO Box 398166, Minneapolis, Minnesota 55439.

Copyright © 2017 by Abdo Consulting Group, Inc. International copyrights reserved in all countries.
No part of this book may be reproduced in any form without written permission from the publisher.

Printed in the United States of America, North Mankato, Minnesota.

052016

092016

THIS BOOK CONTAINS
RECYCLED MATERIALS

Photo Credits: iStock, National Geographic Creative, Science Source, Shutterstock

Production Contributors: Teddy Borth, Jennie Forsberg, Grace Hansen

Design Contributors: Laura Mitchell, Dorothy Toth

Cataloging-in-Publication Data

Names: Hansen, Grace, author.

Title: Becoming a salamander / by Grace Hansen.

Description: Minneapolis, MN : Abdo Kids, [2017] | Series: Changing animals |
     Includes bibliographical references and index.

Identifiers: LCCN 2015959112 | ISBN 9781680805123 (lib. bdg.) |
     ISBN 9781680805680 (ebook) | ISBN 9781680806243 (Read-to-me ebook)

Subjects: LCSH: Salamanders--Juvenile literature. | Life cycles--Juvenile
     literature.

Classification: DDC 597.8--dc23

LC record available at http://lccn.loc.gov/2015959112

Table of Contents

Stage 1

All salamanders begin as eggs.

Most kinds of salamanders lay

eggs in water. Each egg has

a slimy coating.

Stage 2

The eggs hatch after about 30 days. A newly hatched salamander is called a **larva**.

6

7

The larva has a tail. It has a mouth and eyes. It has gills to breathe underwater.

The **larva** eats and grows.
It mostly eats insects. Soon,
the larva begins to grow legs.

11

Stage 3

Months later, the larva has grown into a young salamander. It is able to breathe air. It has fully grown legs. It can walk on land.

The salamander looks for
a cool, moist place. It finds
a forest to call home. Water
will always be nearby.

15

Some salamanders spend their entire lives in water. Others live in caves. They are very pale. They have small eyes. This is because they live in darkness.

Some salamanders grow lungs.

Some keep their **gills**. Most

salamanders have neither.

They breathe through their skin.

Stage 4

The salamander is fully grown.

It has a sticky tongue to catch

prey. It can live for many years.

In that time, it will find a **mate**.

More Facts

- Salamanders mostly come out at night when the sun is down. This is when they do their hunting.

- Different kinds of salamanders eat different things. But typical foods for adult salamanders include crickets, insect eggs and larvae, and worms.

- Salamanders can regrow entire body parts!

Glossary

gills – an organ that takes oxygen out of water.

larva – the early form of an animal that at birth or hatching does not look like its parents and must grow and change to become an adult.

mate – one of a pair of animals that will have young together.

prey – an animal that is hunted for food.

Index

abdokids.com

Use this code to log on to abdokids.com and access crafts, games, videos, and more!

Abdo Kids Code:
CBK5123